Oil Crisis

Gail Riley

www.av2books.com

AV² provides enriched content that supplements and complements this book. Weigl's AV² books strive to create inspired learning and engage young minds in a total learning experience.

Your AV² Media Enhanced books come alive with...

Audio
Listen to sections of the book read aloud.

Key Words
Study vocabulary, and complete a matching word activity.

Video
Watch informative video clips.

Quizzes
Test your knowledge.

Embedded Weblinks
Gain additional information for research.

Slide Show
View images and captions, and prepare a presentation.

Try This!
Complete activities and hands-on experiments.

... and much, much more!

Go to **www.av2books.com**, and enter this book's unique code.

BOOK CODE

Q976886

AV² by Weigl brings you media enhanced books that support active learning.

Download the AV² catalog at **www.av2books.com/catalog**

AV² Online Navigation on page 48

Published by AV² by Weigl
350 5ᵗʰ Avenue, 59ᵗʰ Floor
New York, NY 10118

Website: www.av2books.com www.weigl.com

Library of Congress Control Number: 2013941892
ISBN 978-1-62127-436-0 (hardcover)
ISBN 978-1-62127-442-1 (softcover)
ISBN 978-1-62127-832-0 (single-user eBook)
ISBN 978-1-48961-719-4 (multi-user eBook)

Printed in the United States of America in North Mankato, Minnesota
1 2 3 4 5 6 7 8 9 0 17 16 15 14 13

062013
WEP220513

Weigl acknowledges Getty Images as its primary image supplier for this title.

Every reasonable effort has been made to trace ownership and to obtain permission to reprint copyright material. The publishers would be pleased to have any errors or omissions brought to their attention so that they may be corrected in subsequent printings.

Project Coordinator: Aaron Carr
Art Director: Terry Paulhus

Oil Crisis

CONTENTS

Introduction to Oil

Petroleum, or oil as it is commonly known, is one of the foundations of modern life. Without it, industrial society would grind to a halt. Cars, trucks, trains, aircraft, and ships depend on petroleum products. This reliance on oil presents a number of problems. The world's supply of oil is limited, and most oil is not located in regions where it is used. These factors affect the price and availability of this important product. The **extraction** and use of oil also may cause problems. Oil spills and chemical releases when oil is burned have a major impact on the environment.

Origins of Oil

"It has taken hundreds of millions of years for oil to form far below Earth's surface."

Uses of Oil

"Oil is used every day by people all over the world. It is vital to modern life."

Conflicts Related to Oil

Oil and the Environment

"Many conflicts related to oil have arisen in the Middle East. Conflicts have also occurred in other locations around the world."

"Oil spills and other serious environmental hazards have resulted from oil drilling, transport, and use."

Origins of Oil

KEY CONCEPTS

Oil is located in **deposits** across the world. The oil that exists today was formed long ago and is often far below Earth's surface. Before it can be used by consumers, oil must be located, extracted from the ground, transported, and prepared for use. This is a complex process.

1 Oil Formation

Hundreds of millions of years ago, remains of plants and animals lay on seafloors. These remains mixed with **sedimentary rock**. As time passed, additional sediments built up over the remains. Active volcanoes sent out lava, rock, and ash. Earthquakes also changed the surface of the land.

All of this resulted in a thick, hard layer of rock building up higher and higher over the remains of the plants and animals. The rock created a great deal of pressure and prevented air from passing through.

The pressure and lack of air resulted in bacteria breaking down the animal and plant remains into chemicals called **hydrocarbons**. Oil is made up almost entirely of hydrocarbons. This fuel was formed from the remains of ancient living things, so it is called a fossil fuel.

Some of the oil below Earth's surface collected in huge pools. However, much of the oil deep below the ground today is located in **rock pores**. This oil is not found in large batches, the way water is found in a lake. Instead, it exists as tiny oil droplets stuck to the rock.

Today, all of the rock that covers oil is not airtight. Water and air can get through some of the rock, and the oil can begin to make its way upward. Small amounts of oil can sometimes ooze up out of the ground. Most oil, though, can rise only to a point where it encounters a thick layer of rock below Earth's surface.

At the La Brea Tar Pits in Los Angeles, California, a thick form of petroleum naturally seeps from the ground. Prehistoric animals were trapped in this "tar."

2 Locating Oil

Finding oil has become much easier in recent years. Two hundred years ago, people could locate oil only where it had come up to the surface and trickled across the ground. This was not an effective method of locating oil. It meant people had to wait for the oil to come to them.

During the early 1800s, people drilling for water often discovered oil in the water they sought. They were not looking for the oil, and they were irritated that it destroyed the value of the water they needed. This attitude toward oil changed by the early 1900s, as automobiles replaced horse-drawn vehicles and machines were invented to manufacture goods of all kinds. The new cars and factory machines could not work without fuel, which was made from oil.

New ways of searching for oil became important. One method was finding clues in surface rocks and then starting a well to explore the area below. However, these explorations were often unsuccessful.

Today, more modern methods are used. For example, scientists can drill thousands of feet (meters) below the surface and take **core samples**. They use microscopes to closely inspect the samples. Through the microscopes, they can see whether oil droplets are present in the rock pores.

Scientists also use **3D visualization**. This process provides an image that actually shows the area underground. Drones are increasingly being used as part of 3D visualization. These drones, or planes without pilots, are controlled by scientists giving computer commands from a remote location. The drones contain cameras, **laser scanners**, and **infrared sensors** that gather information about rock far below the surface.

Another method is known as seismic prospecting. Scientists can determine how long it takes sound waves to move through specific underground locations. Computers analyze data to show models of rock formations far below Earth's surface. This helps scientists find oil.

Core samples can tell a scientist about the formation, history, and content of underground rock.

Should the Release of Radiation from Oil Drilling in Azerbaijan Be Investigated?

I n Azerbaijan, a country in southwest Asia, the Apsheron Peninsula is a major oil production area. It is also a region where the rock contains naturally occurring **radioactive** materials, which scientists call NORM.

When the rock is disturbed, such as during oil exploration and drilling, the amount of radiation released from NORM can increase. There is some evidence that NORM radiation is causing health and other problems in the Apsheron Peninsula.

Nongovernmental Organizations (NGOs)
It is important to be able to see the exact effects of oil drilling in this region. We need to determine whether oil companies are doing damage to the people and land in the area.

Environmental Scientists
Oil should not be drilled for profit if this activity is at the expense of people and land. If health problems are occurring for another reason, it is also important to find out what the other cause is.

Oil Workers in Azerbaijan
Oil production creates thousands of jobs and brings income to our region. We are concerned about the environment and people's health. However, we also worry about job loss.

Energy Companies
There is no reason for an investigation. We know that NORM exists in the region and that some radiation can be released as we work. We have safety rules to prevent harmful effects from NORM.

For   Supportive   Undecided   Unsupportive   Against

3 Extracting Oil

After oil has been located, it must be extracted. The first step in this process is to drill a deep hole from the surface to the place where the oil exists. Oil drilling may occur on land or at sea, depending on the location of the oil.

On land, a structure called a derrick is placed at the drilling site. The equipment used for drilling is very heavy, and the derrick provides a platform that will support it. Before drilling begins, a drill bit is placed on a pipe. The bit cuts its way down through the rock to the location of the oil. The oil is pumped up through a hole in the bit into the pipe.

Offshore drilling is used to extract oil from beneath the seafloor. While a derrick is used on land, a drilling platform is used at sea. The platform sometimes has legs that are placed directly on the seafloor. Often, though, the platform floats on the surface, with an anchor running to the ocean floor to hold it in place.

"Devices called blowout preventers are used at drilling sites, so that huge quantities of oil do not gush out all at once."

When oil is finally reached, a great deal of pressure is released. During the early days of drilling for oil, this resulted in huge quantities of oil gushing to the surface. The oil spewed across land, people, and equipment. In the 1920s, new equipment was developed to control the pressure. This equipment has been improved over the years. Devices called blowout preventers are now routinely used at drilling sites, allowing valves to be opened or closed to control the flow of oil. This means that large amounts of oil do not gush out all at once.

Drill bits used by workers on offshore platforms sometimes wear out. When this happens, the pipe must be pulled out. The bit is then replaced, and the drilling can continue.

Should there Be Stricter Laws Regarding Offshore Oil Drilling?

Workers on the Deepwater Horizon offshore platform were drilling an oil well in the Gulf of Mexico in 2010 when an explosion occurred and started a fire. A huge oil spill resulted, causing severe damage to the environment and economy of the U.S. Gulf Coast. Investigations of the accident concluded that it resulted from a combination of human error and faulty equipment. Some people believe that disasters such as the Deepwater Horizon spill would be less likely to occur if there were stricter laws regarding offshore oil drilling.

Some Legislators
The Deepwater Horizon spill shows that oil companies cannot be left to set their own safety policies. They might not follow safety precautions that are very expensive and would reduce their profits. We need tougher laws.

Residents of the Gulf Coast
We suffered huge property losses. Many lost jobs in industries such as fishing and tourism. Accidents can never be totally prevented. However, we want laws that require oil companies to follow strict safety rules.

Oil Workers on the Gulf Coast
We want the environment to be protected. Still, we do not want laws to be so strict that oil companies will not be able to operate. If these companies stop drilling in the Gulf, many jobs will be lost.

Oil Companies
We have learned from past problems, and we will continue to improve our safety procedures. There are already many laws regulating oil companies doing business in the United States. There is no need for more laws.

For	Supportive	Undecided	Unsupportive	Against

4 Transporting Oil

Oil pumped out of the ground is called crude oil. It is not yet usable for powering machinery. Crude oil from a well is transported to a plant called a refinery. There, the crude oil is processed, or refined, into products such as gasoline, heating oil, diesel fuel, and jet fuel.

One common method of transporting oil is through a pipeline. Pipelines often stretch for hundreds or even thousands of miles (kilometers). They move oil efficiently, but they can cause damage to the environment. If a section of a pipeline starts to leak, large amounts of oil may spill out before the problem can be located and fixed.

Huge ships called tankers transport oil across oceans and seas. The biggest of these vessels are called supertankers, and they are among the world's largest ships. A supertanker may carry more than 300,000 tons (272,000 tonnes) of oil. Most often, tankers arrive at their destinations safely. However, oil spills from tanker shipwrecks have harmed fish, sea birds, and other animals living in nearby waters and coastal areas.

Some oil pipelines cross remote, hard-to-reach regions.

562

5 Storing Oil

Crude oil and products made from it are often stored until they are ready for use. Oil can be stored in above-ground tanks. It can also be stored below the ground.

Oil is sometimes even stored in tankers. In 2013, Iran stored oil in tankers in its coastal waters. The United States and many European countries were refusing to buy Iranian oil because they disagreed with the Iranian government's nuclear policy. Iran was not able to sell all of the oil it produced, so it created this floating storage on tankers.

The U.S. government keeps an emergency supply of crude oil called the Strategic Petroleum Reserve (SPR). This oil is stored in **salt caverns** in Texas and Louisiana. These huge caverns occur naturally in the region. They provide a secure and economic way to store oil.

Each of the four SPR storage sites can hold between 6 million and 35 million barrels of oil. A barrel of oil is equal to 42 gallons (160 liters). The SPR storage

sites are connected to a pipeline network for transport across the United States.

Leaks from above-ground or underground oil storage tanks can harm the environment and people's health. The oil that leaks out may contaminate underground water supplies. People and animals drinking this water may become ill.

The U.S. government has issued safety rules that companies must follow to prevent oil spills from storage tanks.

Uses of Oil

KEY CONCEPTS

The oil industry began in the United States in the late 19th century. Its growth was closely tied to development of the automobile industry, since gasoline became the major fuel used for cars. The availability of oil has been important to the growth of many other industries, including **petrochemicals**. Many types of plastic are made from petrochemicals.

1 History of Oil

Early oil wells in Pennsylvania produced oil that was used for **lubricating** machines and lighting lamps. Just as electricity was making **kerosene** lamps obsolete, motor vehicles became popular, especially in the United States. Since their country covered such a large area, people in the United States wanted the freedom cars gave them to go more places and get there faster.

John D. Rockefeller established the Standard Oil Company during the late 1800s. Standard Oil became the most powerful company in the United States, and Rockefeller became one of the richest people in the world. By 1911, U.S. lawmakers decided that Standard Oil controlled too much of the oil industry, and it was split into smaller companies. These smaller companies remained important factors in the world oil industry.

In the first half of the 20th century, the popularity of cars grew in many parts of the world. Affordable gasoline came to be regarded as an essential part of daily life, like water and electricity. People across the world also became dependent on affordable oil for other uses. These included heating homes, powering planes, and making plastic and other products. A handful of large oil companies in **developed countries** controlled global supplies and made vast profits from the oil they pumped. Much of this oil was in **developing countries**. Control over the global oil industry began to change in the second half of the 20th century.

The first successful oil well in the United States was drilled in Titusville, Pennsylvania.

2 U.S. Dependence on Oil

When the United States first began using oil, it produced all the oil it needed. For decades, the country remained self-sufficient in oil. It was not necessary to import from other countries.

This self-sufficiency ended by the 1950s. The country's population grew, and its economy was strong. People had more money to spend on cars and other products. The demand for oil increased. At the same time, some U.S. deposits of oil were starting to get used up. Crude oil production in the United States peaked in 1970. The amount of oil imported was greater than domestic production for the first time in 1998. In 2004, oil imports accounted for 58 percent of U.S. oil consumption. In the late 20th century, much of the oil imported by the United States came from Saudi Arabia and other countries located around the Persian Gulf in the Middle East.

After 2005, the amount of oil imported by the United States began to fall. New technologies, such as **fracking**, allowed companies to extract oil deposits that had been unreachable. Environmentalists were concerned, however, that chemicals used in fracking could get into underground water supplies and cause health problems for people who drink the water.

Oil production increased sharply in areas such as North Dakota. From 2006 to 2012, U.S. oil imports fell by about 20 percent. In the same years, production increased more than 20 percent. The United States was also less dependent than in the past on Persian Gulf countries for its oil imports. In 2011, the United States bought three times as much oil from Canada and Mexico as it did from Saudi Arabia. By 2013, the United States was importing about one-third of the oil that the country was using.

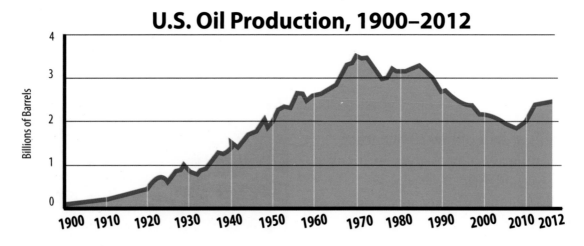

U.S. Oil Production, 1900–2012

Should the Keystone XL Pipeline Be Built?

The Keystone XL Pipeline, designed by a Canadian oil company, is intended to transport oil from Alberta, Canada, through the central United States, to refineries on the Gulf Coast of Texas. If built as planned, the pipeline project would create thousands of construction jobs and some permanent jobs for maintenance workers.

The oil this pipeline would carry is located in deposits called oil sands or tar sands. As found in nature, it is mixed with sand and clay. Scientists say that oil from the oil sands yields less usable energy than other types of oil. There is also some research showing that extracting and using this oil puts more pollutants into the air than using oil from other sources.

Oil Companies
The project will increase the portion of U.S. oil imports that comes from Canada. It is better to get oil from Canada than from areas such as the Middle East, where wars or hostile governments may cut off supplies.

Construction Workers
Thousands of jobs will be created by the pipeline project, at a time when other types of construction jobs are not plentiful. Even if the jobs are temporary, they will help families and the economy in general.

Economists
Many of the jobs created by the project will be temporary construction jobs. Then, the workers will be unemployed. Leaks from the pipeline could be costly to clean up.

Environmentalists
There is great potential for leaks from the pipeline as it carries oil across many states. The refined oil will also make pollution problems worse. We should be looking for alternate energy sources.

For   Supportive   Undecided   Unsupportive   Against

3 Global Dependence on Oil

Many nations around the world depend on oil to meet the energy needs of their people and industries. Developed nations such as Japan and countries in Western Europe have very small supplies of oil. For decades, they have been importing most of the oil they need. Japan imports 99 percent of the oil it uses.

The European Union (EU), a group made up of more than two dozen European countries, imports about 90 percent of its oil. Two-fifths of these imports come from Russia and neighboring countries in Asia. One-fifth comes from the Middle East. Due to their dependence on imports, many European countries passed laws, such as high gasoline taxes, to encourage people to use less oil.

> "Japan imports 99 percent of its oil."

In some countries with rapidly developing economies, the demand for oil has sharply increased in recent years. These countries, including China, India, and Brazil, need more oil for their growing industries. In addition, as people in these countries make more money, they buy more cars that run on gasoline.

China has become the world's second-largest consumer of oil, after the United States. It used more than 9 million barrels of oil per day in 2012. This is about 25 percent higher than just five years earlier.

Worldwide, oil consumption is growing. It increased by more than 10 million barrels per day from 2001 to 2011. Many scientists are concerned about the higher releases of harmful chemicals into the air as more oil is burned each year.

World's Largest Oil Importers, 2011

Country	Millions of Barrels per Day
UNITED STATES	8.81
CHINA	4.58
JAPAN	4.34
INDIA	2.43
GERMANY	2.24
SOUTH KOREA	2.17
FRANCE	1.72
SPAIN	1.36
ITALY	1.30
NETHERLANDS	0.95

Millions of Barrels per Day

4 Global Oil Resources

Large oil deposits are located in various parts of the world, from the Arctic to tropical regions near the equator and the hot deserts of the Middle East. Worldwide, usable **proved reserves** of oil totaled about 1.5 trillion barrels in 2011. That is less than a 50-year supply of oil at the current rate of consumption.

The actual amount of usable oil reserves may be higher. Many remote areas of the world are not yet fully explored. Future advances in technology may make it possible to locate oil that cannot currently be found. New technology may also enable oil companies to extract oil that cannot now be removed from the ground, although there may be harmful environmental effects from these processes.

The usable oil that is known to exist is not evenly distributed. More than half of current proved reserves are in the Middle East. Almost 20 percent of global oil reserves are in just one country, Saudi Arabia. In South America, Venezuela has about 15 percent of the world's oil reserves and is the largest oil producer. Canada's reserves make up about 12 percent of the world total.

Major discoveries of oil have been made in recent years in countries outside the Middle East. For example, large oil deposits have been found in Turkmenistan, Kazakhstan, and Azerbaijan. Pipelines carry the oil out of these countries for export. One of the longest pipelines in the world is the 1,100-mile (1,760-km) Baku-Tbilisi-Ceyhan pipeline. It carries oil from Azerbaijan to Turkey.

Despite the new discoveries, the Middle East remains the world's most important oil-producing region. In addition, even if usable proved reserves increase, the world's supply of oil will not last forever. Especially if oil supplies become less plentiful in the future, there is potential for conflict when a few countries control large amounts of oil.

World's Largest Oil Producers, 2011

(millions of barrels per day)

SAUDI ARABIA	11.15
RUSSIA	10.24
UNITED STATES	10.14
CHINA	4.35
IRAN	4.23
CANADA	3.60
UNITED ARAB EMIRATES	3.01
MEXICO	2.96
KUWAIT	2.69
BRAZIL	2.69
IRAQ	2.63
NIGERIA	2.55
VENEZUELA	2.49
NORWAY	2.01
ALGERIA	1.86

Mapping Oil

Pacific Ocean

14%

North America

Atlantic Ocean

World Oil Reserves, 2011

Some regions of the world are much richer in proved oil reserves than others. This map shows the percentage of the world's oil reserves that are known to exist in different areas. Countries in oil-rich regions are often oil exporters. Countries in other regions often need to import oil.

16%

South America

Legend

- Middle East
- South America, Central America, the Caribbean
- Africa
- United States, Canada, Mexico

- Europe
- Russia, Southwest Asia, Central Asia
- East Asia, Australia, New Zealand

Share of world's proved oil reserves

Arctic Ocean

Europe

1%

Asia

7%

STRAIT OF HORMUZ

51%

3%

Pacific Ocean

Africa

8%

MALACCA STRAIT

Indian Ocean

Australia

Southern Ocean

New
Zealand

N
W   E
S

SCALE   1,200 Miles

1,200 Kilometers

5 Controlling the Supply of Oil

In the 20th century, oil companies based in the United States and Europe explored for oil and developed oil fields in the Middle East and other parts of the world. During the second half of the century, developing countries with oil supplies took action to gain control of their oil resources.

In 1960, four Middle Eastern countries and Venezuela founded the Organization of the Petroleum Exporting Countries (OPEC) to increase their control over the price and supply of oil. Other nations later joined the organization. In the 1970s, some countries, including Saudi Arabia and Venezuela, **nationalized** their oil industries. Also in the 1970s, OPEC members reduced the amount of oil they were producing and sharply increased their prices. For a time, some OPEC members stopped exporting oil to the United States because of U.S. support for Israel in its conflict with Arab countries in the Middle East. Since OPEC, at that time, accounted for as much as 90 percent of global oil exports, it had the power to control the world oil market.

These actions caused temporary shortages and sharp price increases for gasoline, heating oil, and other petroleum products. As a result, the U.S. economy suffered.

The OPEC actions led to changes in U.S. government policy. The United States gave large amounts of financial and military aid to Saudi Arabia, Egypt, and other Middle Eastern countries, to encourage these countries to take actions more favorable to U.S. interests. New laws required U.S. auto companies to produce more fuel-efficient cars.

There was also an increase in exploration for new supplies of oil within the United States and other non-OPEC countries. The trans-Alaska pipeline was built in the 1970s to transport oil from Alaska's North Slope to a tanker port in southern Alaska. In the 21st century, less than half of U.S. oil imports have come from OPEC. Worldwide, OPEC's share of oil exports has fallen to about 60 percent.

When oil exports to the United States were reduced in the 1970s, some drivers waited in line for an hour or more to buy gasoline.

Should Oil Drilling Be Allowed in the Arctic National Wildlife Refuge?

The Arctic National Wildlife Refuge (ANWR) is a protected wilderness area in northern Alaska. Part of ANWR is rich in oil, and other major oil deposits may lie beneath the waters just offshore. Great debate has arisen over whether to allow extensive drilling for oil in this area.

The Arctic is a difficult environment in which to work safely. An accident resulting in a major oil spill could do serious damage to the plant and animal life in the largest protected natural area in the United States.

Oil Companies
This is a rich energy resource we should be using. More domestic oil production will reduce oil prices and lessen U.S. dependence on oil imports. We will exercise great care to protect the environment when we are working in this region.

Oil Workers
Thousands of jobs will be created as a result of oil drilling. People need these jobs. The money workers earn and spend will benefit the economy.

Government Officials
Oil from ANWR can further reduce U.S. dependence on foreign oil. However, we must make sure that there are strict regulations to protect the environment and that the oil companies follow these regulations.

Environmental Groups
There is great danger to the Arctic if drilling is allowed. The operations of oil companies will disturb the natural environment. Oil spills are more likely to occur and more difficult to clean up than in other regions because of the area's harsh climate.

| For | Supportive | Undecided | Unsupportive | Against |

Conflicts Related to Oil

KEY CONCEPTS

Many Middle East oil fields are easy to access. This is important, as productive oil resources in other parts of the world are often less accessible. It is much more difficult to extract and transport oil from areas such as tropical forests and the seafloor.

1 Oil and the Arabian Peninsula

In the Arabian Peninsula, which includes Saudi Arabia and several other countries, oil is often close to the surface beneath barren land. This makes Arabian oil fields ideal for development. Additionally, the pipelines that carry oil across Middle East deserts require very little maintenance. The dry desert conditions cause less long-term damage to pipelines than other types of climates.

The kingdom of Saudi Arabia was established in 1932, after a 30-year effort by Ibn Saud to unify the region. Ibn Saud was the kingdom's first ruler, and his descendants still govern the country today. Important government decisions are made by a handful of members of the royal family.

The United States became involved in Saudi Arabia when the Standard Oil Company began to develop Saudi oil fields in 1933. Although Saudi Arabia participated in the oil **embargo** and price increases of the 1970s, it has often followed policies more favorable to the United States. At times, Saudi Arabia has pressed for higher oil production and lower prices than other OPEC members wanted. Saudi Arabia is the organization's largest oil producer, so it has the greatest influence over OPEC policy.

In 1990, Iraq invaded Saudi Arabia's neighbor Kuwait. Saudi Arabia allied itself with the United States. Hundreds of thousands of U.S. and other troops were based in the country as they prepared to attack Iraqi forces and remove them from Kuwait. The U.S. troops also prevented any Iraqi attack on Saudi Arabia.

Saudi Arabia and five other Arabian Peninsula countries with similar forms of government created the Gulf Cooperation Council (GCC) in 1981. The other members of the council are Bahrain, Kuwait, Oman, Qatar, and the United Arab Emirates. Together, the six GCC countries control more than one-third of the world's proved oil reserves. GCC members work to coordinate their economic and military policies.

Azerbaijan has crude oil reserves totaling about 7 billion barrels.

2 Beyond the Middle East

As of 2011, Russia was the world's second-largest oil producer, after Saudi Arabia. Russia's oil deposits are concentrated in western Siberia and in the Caspian Sea area. There are oil reserves both beneath the land surrounding the Caspian Sea and below the seafloor. Oil exports are important to Russia's economy, and the country is a key supplier of oil to Europe and Israel.

From 1922 to 1991, Russia was part of a larger country called the Union of Soviet Socialist Republics (USSR), or Soviet Union. Except for Iran, the Soviet Union was the only country bordering the Caspian Sea. In 1991, the Soviet Union broke up into 15 separate countries. As a result, three new countries were created that have major oil reserves and border the Caspian Sea. These countries are Azerbaijan, Kazakhstan, and Turkmenistan.

National boundaries in the Caspian Sea are not well defined. There have been disputes among the bordering nations over who owns some of the oil deposits below the seafloor. For example, three oil fields in the Caspian Sea are claimed by both Azerbaijan and Turkmenistan. Iran has also drilled for oil in a part of the sea Azerbaijan claims. In addition, Russia has opposed pipeline projects to transport oil from Azerbaijan or Kazakhstan without passing through Russia. Such projects could help the former Soviet states sell oil at a lower price than Russia.

Disputes have not yet turned into armed conflicts. However, some countries in the region are using their new oil wealth to build up their military strength. In the first decade of the 21st century, Azerbaijan increased its military spending by 471 percent, and Kazakhstan by 360 percent.

Should the United States Help some Countries Build up their Navies in the Caspian Sea?

Russia and Iran have long had navy warships based in the Caspian Sea. In recent years, Azerbaijan, Kazakhstan, and Turkmenistan have started to build or increase the size of their own navies in this sea.

The three countries want the United States to supply them with ships and other military equipment. They argue that, by doing this, the United States can help protect an important part of the world's valuable oil supplies and keep its rivals Russia and Iran from becoming too powerful.

U.S. Military
This is an important oil-rich region of the world, and the United States should provide military assistance. One or two powerful countries should not be able to control more oil than they really own.

Western Oil Companies
We are working with these three countries to help them develop their oil resources and transport oil to Europe and other markets. They should be able to sell their oil in order to increase global oil supplies.

Some U.S. Legislators
We want oil development to continue, and we want oil to be available. However, we do not think the United States should be involved in military disputes between far-off countries.

Some U.S. Taxpayers
We do not believe the United States should spend money to help other countries build up their navies. There are many important economic needs at home that should be addressed. Our taxes can only pay for so much.

 For   Supportive   Undecided   Unsupportive   Against

3 Conflicts with Iran

Two Middle Eastern countries with extensive oil supplies are Iran and Iraq. These countries border each other, and both have coastlines on the Persian Gulf. Each country has almost 10 percent of the world's proved oil reserves.

Most people in both countries are Muslims, or followers of the Islamic faith. However, a majority of Iraqis are Sunni Muslims, while most Iranians are Shiite Muslims. Sunnis and Shiites disagree on some important religious teachings.

From the 1950s to 1970s, Muhammad Reza Pahlavi, who had the title shah of Iran, ruled the country as a dictator. The United States supported the shah's government and purchased oil from Iran. The U.S. government also sold Iran military equipment.

Opposition in Iran to the shah's harsh rule increased in the 1970s, and violent protests forced him to leave the country in 1979. A government controlled by Shiite religious leaders took power. Iran's new rulers were hostile to the United States because it had supported the shah. In late 1979, Iranian protesters took over the U.S. embassy in Tehran, Iran's capital city. More than 50 Americans were held hostage for 444 days.

In 2005, the U.S. government accused Iran of secretly developing nuclear weapons. To pressure Iran to change its policy, the United Nations in 2006 voted to impose economic **sanctions** on Iran. Sanctions have recently become tougher, and many countries refuse to trade with Iran. These steps have severely hurt the Iranian economy.

Iran has threatened to block the Strait of Hormuz, the narrow waterway that connects the Persian Gulf to the ocean. This could have a major effect on world oil supplies, since a great deal of Middle East oil is shipped to the rest of the world through the Persian Gulf. The United States has sent warships to the Gulf to try to prevent any blockage of the Strait of Hormuz.

Iranian protesters who took over the U.S. embassy in 1979 burned American flags to show their opposition to the United States.

4 Conflicts with Iraq

For more than two decades beginning in 1979, Iraq's government was headed by President Saddam Hussein. He ruled as a dictator and put down all opposition to his government, including that from the Kurdish ethnic group and from the country's Shiite Muslim minority. Iraq attacked Iran in 1980, and the two countries fought an eight-year war. Both countries' oil exports declined during the war. The United States and some European countries sold weapons to Iraq in the 1980s.

U.S. policy toward Iraq changed after Saddam Hussein invaded oil-rich Kuwait and appeared to threaten Saudi Arabia in 1990. A U.S.-led coalition that included troops from many other nations pushed Iraqi forces out of Kuwait in 1991. Retreating Iraqi troops severely damaged Kuwaiti oil fields and equipment. Both the Iran-Iraq war and the Kuwaiti invasion were reminders of the potential for conflict in the Middle East to disrupt world oil supplies.

On September 11, 2001, members of the Islamic terrorist group Al-Qaeda attacked targets in the United States. Soon after, the U.S. government accused Iraq of supporting terrorism. U.S. government officials also claimed that Iraq was developing or was increasing its production of weapons of mass destruction (WMDs). These WMDs were said to include nuclear bombs and **chemical weapons**. In 2003, U.S. troops invaded Iraq and removed Hussein from power. Stores of WMDs were not found.

Years of conflict in Iraq followed Hussein's overthrow. Kurdish, Shiite, Sunni, and Islamic extremist groups fought against each other for power and against the thousands of U.S. troops that remained in the country. Elections in 2010 brought a new Iraqi government into office, and the level of violence declined. The last U.S. troops left the country the following year. Iraqi oil production declined sharply in the early 2000s, but it was steadily recovering by 2012.

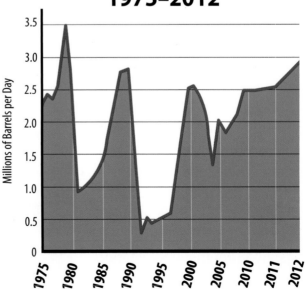

Iraq's Oil Production, 1975–2012

5 Threats to the Oil Supply

Every day, tens of millions of barrels of oil are transported through a worldwide system of pipelines, tankers, and trucks. This system provides potential targets for terrorists and other groups trying to hurt the economies of the United States and other countries.

Tankers are especially vulnerable to attack when the ships must pass through narrow channels, such as the Strait of Hormuz. This waterway is less than 25 miles (40 km) wide. About one-fifth of all the oil traded worldwide moves through the strait.

Another vulnerable shipping channel is the Strait of Malacca in Asia. Located between the Malay Peninsula and the Indonesian island of Sumatra, the strait is only 40 miles (65 km) wide at its narrowest point. It provides the shortest route from the Middle East to Japan, China, and other countries in East Asia, so the strait is used by many tankers. Security for ships in the Strait of Malacca is largely provided by Indonesia, Malaysia, and Singapore. Japan has given financial assistance for security efforts.

To make it less vulnerable to attack, the Baku-Tbilisi-Ceyhan pipeline in southwest Asia was constructed below ground, rather than above. Security measures include cameras, electronic sensors, and floodlights along the pipeline route. Walls were built to prevent trucks carrying explosives from reaching the pipeline.

> "Pipelines, tankers, and trucks that carry oil provide potential targets for terrorists."

The Department of Homeland Security (DHS) is the government agency that is responsible for the security of oil pipelines in the United States. Actual protection of these pipelines is largely conducted by the private companies that own and operate them. The DHS issues regulations that these companies must follow. The agency also alerts companies to any potential attacks the government becomes aware of.

To prevent attacks, U.S. or European navy ships sometimes escort tankers sailing through the Strait of Hormuz.

Does Iran Have a Right to Stop Tanker Traffic in the Strait of Hormuz?

After tough economic sanctions against Iran went into effect, the country's oil sales fell sharply. Government officials in Iran, angry over the impact on their economy, said that Iran might stop tankers from taking other countries' oil exports out of the Persian Gulf through the strait. The Strait of Hormuz borders Iran, which has navy ships in the region. This means that countries exporting or importing oil through the strait take very seriously the Iranian threats to interfere with tanker traffic.

Iranian Officials
We have a right to protect our own interests. Other countries imposed sanctions on Iran that have had a negative impact on our economy. We should be able to take actions that hurt their economies, to try to convince them to stop the sanctions.

Oil Workers in Iran
We do not want our government to take actions that might start a war. However, if Iran cannot sell oil, our jobs are threatened. We also have pride in our country. We do not want other countries telling us what to do.

Oil-importing Countries
We do not want to have an armed conflict. However, we cannot allow any country to block a large part of the world's oil shipments. The economy of the whole world depends on reliable supplies of oil.

Some Legal Experts
Iran has no legal right to close the Strait of Hormuz. This waterway is considered part of international waters. For centuries, nations around the world have agreed that ships of all countries have the right to pass freely through international waters.

 For   Supportive   Undecided   Unsupportive   Against

Oil and the Environment

Most scientists believe the world should prepare for a time when oil is no longer widely available. They are also concerned that creating and using petroleum products affects the environment in many ways.

1 Renewable Energy

Many people believe the United States and the world should reduce their reliance on oil by making greater use of **renewable energy sources**. Oil is a **nonrenewable energy source**. In the future, the world will not be able to depend on oil the way it does today.

While the world continues to rely on oil, burning gasoline and other petroleum products is releasing **carbon dioxide** into the air. Carbon dioxide is a **greenhouse gas**. Many scientists believe that an increasing amount of carbon dioxide in Earth's atmosphere is a major cause of **climate change**. The warming of Earth's climate is causing drought in some areas and flooding in others.

Using renewable energy sources does not add carbon dioxide to the atmosphere. Major renewable sources include wind, water, and solar power. The force of the wind or flowing water can be used to turn engines called turbines, producing electricity. Solar panels convert the energy in sunlight into electricity. Electricity from renewable sources can be used to recharge the batteries that power electric cars, which burn no gasoline.

2 Oil Spills

Oil spills are fairly rare occurrences. In the United States, oil companies must follow government safety rules that help prevent oil spills. However, when a spill occurs, it can have a huge impact on the environment.

The largest U.S. tanker spill occurred in 1989 when the *Exxon Valdez* struck a reef in Prince William Sound near the south coast of Alaska. More than 11 million gallons (42 million L) of oil spilled out of the tanker. There were huge losses to wildlife. In 1990, Congress passed a law requiring stricter safety precautions for tankers.

The largest oil spill at a drilling site followed the 2010 explosion at the Deepwater Horizon offshore platform. More than 200 million gallons (750 million L) of oil spilled into the Gulf of Mexico. Eleven workers died in the explosion, and the oil spill caused billions of dollars in losses to the regional economy.

Especially after years of use, oil pipelines can develop leaks. For example, in 2013, a 60-year-old pipeline in Arkansas began leaking. More than 7,000 barrels of oil spilled into a residential area.

3 The Power of the Oil Industry

Oil companies are among the largest corporations in the world. They are also some of the most profitable companies. Especially after a major oil spill, many people become concerned that these companies are too powerful and that their activities should be more strictly controlled by governments

Oil companies say their large profits are justified because the companies also have high costs and take big risks. For example, it is very expensive to explore for oil in remote regions. These areas may have harsh climates and other difficult working conditions. Sometimes, a company will not find oil in a region where it is exploring. In that case, the company gets no benefit for the money it spent on exploration. If oil is found, it may be very costly to extract and transport that oil to refineries.

The companies also face political risks. In some parts of the world, war or other violence can disrupt a company's operations and even put its workers in danger. Another risk is that the government of a country where an oil company is drilling may take over the company's operations.

Company officials maintain that the oil industry is providing a product that people want and that modern society needs in order to function. For this reason, these officials believe their companies should be able to explore and drill wherever large supplies of oil may exist. Other people favor a more limited approach. They believe that, even if oil is an essential product, certain areas should be off limits to drilling. These places include **wetlands**, where just the activity of drilling may disrupt the environment and where a spill can cause very serious environmental damage.

World's Largest Oil and Gas Companies, 2012

(average production per day for the largest companies that are not government-owned)

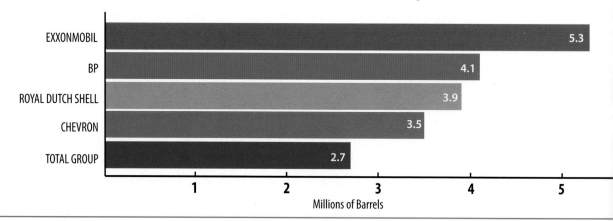

Company	Millions of Barrels
EXXONMOBIL	5.3
BP	4.1
ROYAL DUTCH SHELL	3.9
CHEVRON	3.5
TOTAL GROUP	2.7

Should Laws Be Passed to Keep Oil Platforms Away from Wetlands?

Wetlands located along seacoasts are important to the environment. During severe storms, they help to protect inland areas against flooding. They also prevent soil erosion because they absorb the energy of coastal tides. Without wetlands, these tides would wash away soil.

Wetlands are highly vulnerable to damage from oil spills in nearby waters. Tides can cause oil to repeatedly wash onto, under, and around plants and animals. Oil-covered living things cannot get the air and food they need to survive.

Environmentalists
Yes, oil platforms should be forced farther away from wetlands. Accidents and leaks can be devastating to these areas. Wetlands have so many useful functions that protecting them should be a top priority for everyone.

Botanists
As scientists who study plants, we know that many types of plants found in wetlands are easily harmed or killed by an oil spill. We understand that the world needs oil, but protecting our planet's plant life is also important.

Citizens
We enjoy the beauty of wetlands and do not want to see them destroyed. However, we also understand the need for oil. If safety rules were made stricter, perhaps it would not be necessary to prohibit drilling near wetlands.

Some Business Leaders
The health of our economy depends on having oil available at a reasonable price. If we limit oil drilling, and the price of oil goes up, then the costs of running a business increase.

For	Supportive	Undecided	Unsupportive	Against

Oil through History

The first oil well was not drilled until the middle of the 19th century, and oil has been an important product for not much more than 100 years. In that time, however, it has transformed the way people live, work, and travel. It has become so important that wars have been fought over oil. In addition, it is likely that the use of oil has changed Earth's environment in major ways.

1859
In Titusville, Pennsylvania, Edwin Drake drills the first producing oil well.

1870
John D. Rockefeller enters the oil-refining business and forms Standard Oil to produce kerosene for lighting purposes.

1896
The invention of the gasoline-powered automobile creates a new need for oil.

1870

1901
The first oil well in Texas, called Spindletop, begins production.

1901

1910
Large-scale oil production begins in Mexico.

1933
Standard Oil drills for petroleum in the deserts of Saudi Arabia.

1960
The Organization of the Petroleum Exporting Countries is established.

1973
An embargo on oil sales to the United States by some Middle Eastern countries causes gasoline shortages and higher fuel prices.

1977
The trans-Alaska pipeline opens, to transport oil from northern Alaska to the port of Valdez on Alaska's south coast, where it is loaded onto tankers.

1980–1988

War between Iraq and Iran disrupts oil supplies.

1989

The *Exxon Valdez* tanker hits a reef off the coast of southern Alaska, causing a huge oil spill that affects animal life and the region's environment.

2003

Oil prices rise as a result of the U.S.-led military action in Iraq.

2006

The Baku-Tbilisi-Ceyhan oil pipeline begins to operate. It carries oil from Azerbaijan to the Turkish port of Ceyhan, located on the Mediterranean Sea.

2010

BP Deepwater Horizon Oil Spill and Offshore Drilling

William Reilly

Sen. Bob Graham

2006

The United Nations imposes economic sanctions on Iran.

2008

New technology allows large-scale oil extraction to begin in North Dakota, which soon becomes one of the biggest U.S. oil-producing states.

2010

The Deepwater Horizon oil spill in the Gulf of Mexico causes severe environmental and economic damage along the U.S. Gulf Coast.

2012

Iran's oil exports drop sharply as a result of economic sanctions.

1989

Working with Oil

PETROLEUM ENGINEER

Duties Plan and supervise oil exploration and drilling operations

Education A bachelor's or master's degree in engineering, geology, geophysics, tectonics, or mining

Interest Exploring, drilling, and extracting oil

Petroleum engineers are involved in all phases of oil exploration and extraction. The typical petroleum engineer works in the field. He or she identifies sites that have a strong likelihood of containing oil. Then, samples are taken from the site to determine the amount of oil, how deep below the surface it is, and what equipment will be needed to extract it. The petroleum engineer supervises construction and operations at the site. Petroleum engineers use computer models to help them determine the best way to extract the oil at each site. They must be able to identify, analyze, and solve problems. Petroleum engineers must also be able to communicate well.

OIL WELL FIREFIGHTER

Duties Put out oil well fires

Education Firefighters receive specialized training when they begin work

Interest Providing public service

Oil well fires and other emergencies can take lives and destroy property. Firefighters help deal with these dangers. They must often make quick decisions in risky situations. An oil well firefighter's job is challenging and dangerous. No two oil well fires are alike. Firefighters must know how to follow the correct procedures to fight the blaze. Oil well fires can be unpredictable. Courage, endurance, and strength are among the personal qualities oil well firefighters must possess.

LAND SURVEYOR

Duties Use records and technical equipment to figure out boundaries

Education A bachelor's degree in engineering, geology, or geophysics

Interest Working outdoors, using global positioning systems (GPS) and other equipment

Before an oil well can be drilled, a land surveyor maps out the drilling area and draws up a detailed plan of the site. The plan shows the site's boundaries and the location of equipment within it. The surveyor must check legal documents. He or she must make sure that all drilling activities take place within the legal boundaries of the site.

DERRICK OPERATOR

Duties Prepare, operate, inspect, and repair drilling equipment

Education A high school diploma

Interest Working to drill for oil

Derrick operators work at drilling sites. They prepare the drilling equipment to be used. They also make frequent inspections of the equipment while it is in use. A derrick operator repairs items as necessary. Derrick operators usually receive their job training on drilling sites. They often begin work as roustabouts. A roustabout does many types of labor at a site, helping a derrick operator with a variety of tasks. After the roustabout becomes skilled, he or she may be promoted to the position of derrick operator.

Key Oil Organizations

OPEC

Goal Set production levels for member countries and influence oil prices

Reach Worldwide

Facts Has 12 member countries that together have more than three-fourths of the world's oil reserves

The Organization of the Petroleum Exporting Countries (OPEC) is an international organization made up of some of the world's largest oil producers. It was created in 1960 at a conference in Iraq. OPEC members try to agree on how much oil each member will produce each year. The organization tries to keep oil prices at a level that brings in high income for member countries.

OECD

Goal Cooperate to solve economic issues facing member nations and improve the economies of developing nations

Reach Worldwide

Facts 34 member countries in Europe, North America, and other regions

The Organization for Economic Cooperation and Development (OECD) was established in 1960. It researches economic trends and problems facing countries around the word, including issues related to the supply and price of oil. The organization works with governments to develop solutions to common economic problems.

Luis E. Echáva
Director-General, OECD

EPA

Goal Prevent and deal with environmental problems

Reach United States

Facts U.S. government agency mainly responsible for responding to oil spills within the United States

The Environmental Protection Agency (EPA) enforces laws and issues safety rules intended to prevent oil spills in the United States. It oversees oil drilling in inland waters, as well as on land. The agency also develops plans for responding to oil spills, and it trains workers who clean up spills when they occur. The EPA is one of two government agencies dealing with U.S. oil spills. The Coast Guard responds to oil spills in deepwater ports and coastal waters.

IEA

Goal Ensure a reliable supply of affordable energy for its 28 members

Reach Worldwide

Facts Established to respond to the oil shortages and price increases of the early 1970s

The International Energy Agency (IEA) focuses on four main areas, one of which is energy security. It conducts research, analyzes data, and makes recommendations to its members regarding ways to protect oil supplies and prevent oil price increases. Its members are developed nations, most of which import oil.

Research an Oil Issue

The Issue

Oil is a subject of much debate. Groups may not always agree on the best ways to protect or run oil operations. It is important to enter a discussion to hear all the points of view before making decisions. Discussing issues will ensure that the actions taken are beneficial for all involved.

Get the Facts

Choose an issue (Political, Cultural, Economic, or Ecological) from this book. Then, pick one of the four groups presented in the issue spectrum. Using the book and research in the library or on the Internet, find out more about the group you chose. What is important to members of this group? Why are they backing or opposing the particular issue? What claims or facts can they use to support their point of view? Be sure to write clear and concise supporting arguments for your group. Focus on oil and the ways the group's needs relate to it. Will this group be affected in a positive or negative way by action taken related to oil?

Use the Concept Web

A concept web is a useful research tool. Read the information and review the structure in the concept web on the next page. Use the relationships between concepts to help you understand your group's point of view.

Organize Your Research

Sort your information into organized points. Make sure your research clearly answers the impact the issue will have on your chosen group, how that impact will affect the group, and why the group has chosen the specific point of view.

OIL CONCEPT WEB

Use this concept web to understand the network of factors contributing to issues related to oil.

- Rigs drill for oil located deep below the ground or seafloor.
- Some oil is very hard to reach or extract.
- Technology makes locating and extracting oil easier than in the past.

- Popularity of cars in the 20th century spurred the need for oil.
- Nations around the world rely on oil for transportation, industry, and heating.
- Plastics and other chemicals are made from oil.

- Oil formation began hundreds of millions of years ago.
- Remains of plants and animals broke down, forming hydrocarbons.

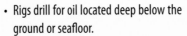

Extracting Oil

Origins of Oil

Uses of Oil

Oil Crisis

Conflicts Related to Oil

Oil and the Environment

Supplies of Oil

- Wars in oil-producing countries can disrupt oil supplies.
- Countries can refuse to sell oil to other nations because of policy disputes.
- Countries disagree about pipeline routes.
- Shipping routes for oil may be vulnerable to attack.

- Oil supplies are not evenly distributed around the world.
- More than half of known oil reserves are in the Middle East.
- Countries that use more oil than they have available within their own boundaries must import from other nations.
- Oil-producing countries have power over supply and price.

- Oil is a nonrenewable energy source.
- When oil is burned, carbon dioxide is released into the air.
- Oil use may contribute to climate change.
- Accidents at drilling sites and during transportation of oil can damage the environment.

Test Your Knowledge

Answer each of the questions below to test your knowledge of oil issues.

1 Why is oil called a fossil fuel?

2 What is seismic prospecting?

3 Why does oil no longer gush to the surface when a petroleum deposit is first hit during drilling?

4 Where did the Deepwater Horizon oil spill occur?

5 What is the SPR?

6 What U.S. oil company began drilling for oil in Saudi Arabia in 1933?

7 What do the initials OPEC stand for?

8 Who are the six members of the Gulf Cooperation Council?

9 What agency is mainly responsible for the security of oil pipelines in the United States?

10 What are three renewable energy sources?

ANSWERS 1. It was formed from the remains of living things. **2.** Seismic prospecting is a method of searching for oil using sound waves. **3.** New technology, such as the blowout preventer, controls the pressure. **4.** The Gulf of Mexico **5.** The Strategic Petroleum Reserve, which holds supplies of oil the United States can use in an emergency **6.** Standard Oil **7.** Organization of the Petroleum Exporting Countries **8.** Bahrain, Kuwait, Oman, Qatar, Saudi Arabia, and the United Arab Emirates **9.** The Department of Homeland Security **10.** Solar, wind, and water power

44 • Global Issues

Key Words

3D visualization: a method to locate oil through seeing a three-dimensional image of an area below the ground

carbon dioxide: an odorless, colorless gas that is a part of Earth's atmosphere and that is produced when fossil fuels are burned

chemical weapons: weapons that release toxic substances that can kill people and other living things and harm the environment

climate change: a change in average temperatures and other weather conditions over a long period of time, such as the major warming trend that most scientists agree has been taking place over the past century

core samples: sections of rock or other material drilled from underground

deposits: layers of material

developed countries: countries that have strong economies and advanced industries

developing countries: countries with low average income that until recently had little manufacturing and technology

embargo: a refusal by one country to trade with or sell products to another country

extraction: removal

fracking: a drilling technique that uses liquid under high pressure to release oil from rocks far below ground

greenhouse gas: a gas in the atmosphere that traps heat near Earth's surface, much as the glass walls of a greenhouse trap heat inside

hydrocarbons: substances made up of the elements hydrogen and carbon

infrared sensors: devices that measure the heat energy radiating from objects

kerosene: a hydrocarbon refined from petroleum

laser scanners: devices that create an image of an object by measuring the time it takes an intense beam of light to reach and bounce back from the object

lubricating: making slippery, such as lubricating the parts of a machine, so that they do not scrape against each other

nationalized: action by a government to take control of an industry away from private companies and run the industry itself

nonrenewable energy source: a resource that exists in limited amounts and will be used up over time

petrochemicals: chemicals that are made from petroleum or natural gas

proved reserves: oil deposits that are known to exist and have not been extracted

radioactive: substances that give off potentially harmful tiny particles because the nuclei of their atoms break down

renewable energy sources: resources available in unlimited quantities in nature

rock pores: tiny holes inside rocks

salt caverns: large caves containing major salt deposits

sanctions: steps taken by a country or group of countries to influence another nation to stop a certain policy or action

sedimentary rock: rock composed of small bits of clay, silt, sand, or other materials

wetlands: areas where water covers soil or is located at or near the soil's surface

Index

Log on to www.av2books.com

AV² by Weigl brings you media enhanced books that support active learning. Go to www.av2books.com, and enter the special code found on page 2 of this book. You will gain access to enriched and enhanced content that supplements and complements this book. Content includes video, audio, weblinks, quizzes, a slide show, and activities.

AV² Online Navigation

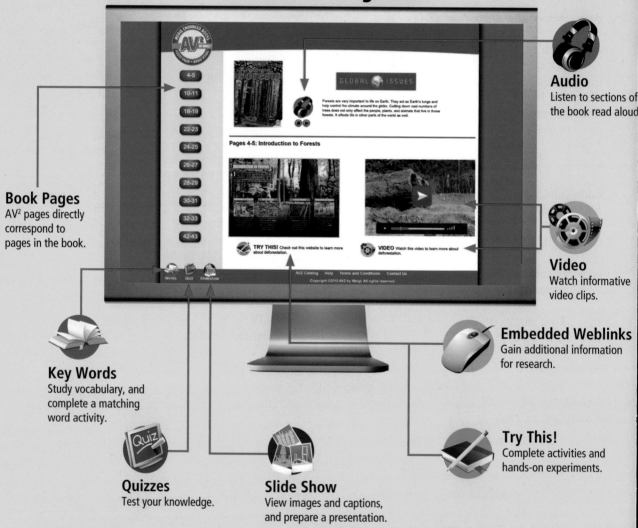

Audio
Listen to sections of the book read aloud

Book Pages
AV² pages directly correspond to pages in the book.

Video
Watch informative video clips.

Key Words
Study vocabulary, and complete a matching word activity.

Embedded Weblinks
Gain additional information for research.

Quizzes
Test your knowledge.

Slide Show
View images and captions, and prepare a presentation.

Try This!
Complete activities and hands-on experiments.

AV² was built to bridge the gap between print and digital. We encourage you to tell us what you like and what you want to see in the future.

Sign up to be an AV² Ambassador at www.av2books.com/ambassador.